BIBLICAL INTERPRETATION OF HEADSHIP IN MARRIAGE

God's Demand from every Christian Husband

SAMUEL DANIEL

DEDICATION

To God, the Institutor of marriage;

To every Christian husband who strives to love
their wives as Christ loves the Church, and;

To every man who desires to raise godly seeds
and build a home where Christ is reverenced
and served, this book is dedicated.

TABLE OF CONTENTS

INTRODUCTION

"For the husband is the head of the wife, even as Christ is the head of the church: and he is the saviour of the body" (Eph. 5:23).

In October 2024, I was interviewed by a business networking organisation in one of the leading cities in Nigeria. During the interview, I learned that a gentleman was occupying the position I applied for. However, he would be retrenched because he wasn't meeting the company's expectations. As a community lead, the gentleman failed to drive his team to generate enough force to scale up sales. Unfortunately, he had to lose his job. That was a lesson for me.

An organisation will only thrive when a correct headship system is in place. A poor leader plus a good team will make up an unproductive system. This is so because the head of any organisation is the driver of its success or failure. Similarly, every Christian husband occupies a strategic and indispensable position in marriage. To despise the office of a husband is to imply that a head is insignificant to its body.

Every man who owns a family has a headship role conferred on him. You either 'drive sales' or get sacked. Although God will not sack you and give your wife to another man, He rewards every work- good or evil.

As a husband, you signed your new office as the head of your home when you made your marriage vows at the altar. You so did before the Lord, and you were witnessed by the congregation of other saints in Christ. So, as the head of your home, God will hold you accountable for your actions or inactions.

Beyond the appellation of headship, a good understanding of the responsibilities attached will help every Christian husband to focus on their primary assignment in marriage. Moreover, you can become a better husband when you understand God's job description for the marriage He instituted.

This book enlightens Christian husbands on headship within the confines of marriage. Additionally, it provides the biblical interpretation and implication of accepting to be a husband. You seek knowledge that will polish and refine you as a Christian husband. May you find this book a suitable guidepost.

CHAPTER 1
DEMYSTIFIED MYSTERY

How do you explain to a naïve child that yesterday was Sunday, and you told her again that yesterday was Tuesday on Wednesday? You may get her more confused if you try to explain that the day before today is yesterday and that the day after today is tomorrow. She might not be able to comprehend that every day on the calendar can be yesterday, today, or tomorrow, depending on certain contexts.

For a layperson, the sun travels from the east to the west. But advanced knowledge explains that the sun is static; it is the earth that revolves around it. It's unbelievable for some folks to accept that the earth rotates daily. "I have never found myself in another location or found my house missing when I return from farm," a layman once questioned.

Several mysteries exist in God's realms that human wisdom cannot fathom. Only as we become God's children do we begin to access the mysteries of His kingdom. To every growing child of God, the mysteries of Christ unfold gradually. Today, we are no longer in doubt that Christ's substitutionary sacrifice on the cross of Calvary guarantees our eternal salvation. For the unbelieving, the redemption story remains a mystery and myth.

Unraveling the Mystery

For the vast majority, marriage is best described as the union between a legally married man and a woman. Others esteem it as a decision every mature man and woman should make. However, a few people picture marriage as a multifaceted institution that has puzzled humans for centuries. It is enshrined in such mysteries that no scholar has been able to unravel. God made it so.

There is no way to describe an institution God established by engaging our limited human wisdom. The best philosophers and theorists would remain shallow in their definition of marriage until God lightens it up. I found in Scripture that marriage is a similitude of the relationship between Christ and His church. It dazzles me now and again.

"This is a profound mystery- but I am speaking about Christ and the church"- Ephesians 5:32.

One of the commonest scriptures read while solemnising holy matrimony is Ephesians 5:22-33. Most dedicated Christians understand that it is one of the Bible passages that teach about marriage at length. However, as much as we can glean eternal wisdom that can fortify our marriages from the passage, Apostle Paul ended by clarifying to the recipients of the letter that marriage is a symbol of the relationship between Christ and His church.

Simply put, marriage is God's parable of the relationship between Christ and the saints. First, God wants us to understand the union between Him and Christ and the intimacy between Him and His church. Does that make any sense to you?

Marriage physically demonstrates the spiritual union between Christ and his church. So, if pagans do not know the depth of God's love for us, our marriage should mirror it to them. How you love your wife as a husband should paint a faint picture of Christ loving His church.

You see, Christ knows how dumb worldly people are. He knows that they are dull of understanding. It takes the spiritual to understand spiritual things. But God also wants to win the natural and logical people to Himself. For this reason, most of Christ's teachings were conveyed in parables. Christ used earthly stories to drive spiritual meanings so that our understanding could be enlightened.

Marriage is one such physical illustration of a spiritual matter. God wants every Christian husband to behave with their wives as Christ would act with His church. Whatever Christ will not do to His church is forbidden for any husband to do to her wife. Any Christian husband who lacks the attributes of Christ in his home will undoubtedly exhibit a false picture of Christ to the church.

Although you cannot take the place of Christ in your home, pictorially, you should be to your wife what Christ is to the church. Otherwise, you will miss God's purpose for the Christian marriage.

As we seek biblical understanding of headship in marriage, we must consult the Scriptures. The story begins in the book of Genesis, where we see God primarily laying down the defined order of creation. Genesis 2:18 reads, "The Lord God said, 'It is not good for the man to be alone. I will make a helper suitable for him."

This is the first Scripture about the idea of a marriage relationship. In this sense, the word "helper" does not refer to a lower or inferior position; instead, it appreciates the unique contributions of both partners to the success of their relationship.

The New Testament reestablishes this perspective. In Ephesians 5:22-33, one considers the great mystery of the relationship between Christ and the Church, in which the man is commanded to love his wife as Christ loved the Church – to die for her. This then lays the foundation of headship- not being abusive in authority but lovingly understanding and taking responsibility.

Most people erroneously interpret headship as a dominance in the hierarchy that offers authority at the expense of subjugation. Nevertheless, upon further study of the scriptures, it becomes clear that a good head is a loving, sacrificing servant leader like Jesus.

Ephesians 5:25-28 illustrates this principle when it tells husbands to love their wives as Christ loves the church, without thinking of themselves, but giving themselves completely for her.

This kind of love does not mean trying to dominate the other person; it means protecting and respecting one's partner and caring for them. Comprehending this theocentric conception of headship is critical to combat stereotypes and redeem the respect due to the headship position.

Adopting Christ's Attitude

"Your attitude should be the same as that of Christ Jesus" – Philippians 2:5.

Since every Christian husband is a physical reflection of Christ in their home, we should see the traits of Christ in them. The only way to prove that we belong to Christ and reflect His image is to do the exact things He did and live the same way He lived. Believers were first called Christians in Antioch because they operated like Christ (Acts 11:26). Their character and ways of life were traceable to Christ. They represented Christ well, and so must every Christian husband.

Christ was selfless. He served humanity at the expense of His comfort and pleasure. As the Saviour of the world, we expect Christ to build an empire where people from diverse cultures and races will come with presents before they can access Him. However, instead of waiting for sinners to come to Him, He went out preaching the kingdom of God. Instead of waiting for sick folks to find their way to Him, He went about doing good and healing all that were oppressed by demons (Acts 10:38).

Humility is one of Christ's attributes that steers at my face. After a miracle service, He would seek a hideout. Sometimes, he scolded demons and commanded them to hold their peace; otherwise, they would herald who He was. Why would Jesus heal the sick and charge them not to tell anyone?

After x-raying my life at a certain time, the Holy Spirit found pride and convicted me. I thought I was humble enough, but I became defensive. But I became broken when the Holy Spirit whispered: "The humility of Christ is the scale for measuring pride." I admitted at once and cried for help.

Most of the miracles Jesus did were spurred by compassion. He was quick to have mercy on sinners. He healed the sick by mercy and associated with the lowly. His compassion does not fail.

He forgives even those we would call the unforgivable. He died for us, not when we acknowledged our sins, but while we were sinners (Rom. 5:8). He offered Himself as the sacrifice for our sins ever before we admit them. What love!

We can go on and on listing Christ's wonderful characters. Most importantly, every Christian husband should have the same attitude that Christ exhibited. Be a compassionate, humble, forgiving, and sacrificial husband. When you demonstrate these qualities, it won't be difficult for your wife and children to understand how Christ loves them.

CHAPTER 2
BIBLICAL INTERPRETATION OF HEADSHIP

Cultural and societal systems have warped the orientation of several men. Heartaches become inevitable when we neglect what the Bible says to follow what we believe is right. Many of the problems people battle in marriage are because they are impervious to scriptural guidelines.

That society exhibits headship in a particular way does not make it right. Besides, culture is not superior to Scripture. Our blueprint is the Bible; until we get back to it, we may keep treading the wrong path.

Some cultural values do not align with Scripture; hence, they should be discarded. God instituted marriage; only He can accurately describe a husband's role and office.

It's time we held the word of God in high esteem and placed it above all human philosophy. By worldly standards, a head is a boss, but that is not scriptural. So, let's study what headship in marriage truly means.

A Symbolism of Christ's Headship

"For the husband is the head of the wife as Christ is the head of the church, his body, of which he is the Savior"- Ephesians 5:23

Whatever God institutes must take its bearing from Him. First, headship in marriage symbolises Christ's headship over the church. Every husband is the head of his wife, like Christ is the head of the church. So, marriage affords every Christian husband the privilege to act like Christ and every godly wife the opportunity to behave like a healthy church.

Just as the church is the body of Christ, every husband is the head of his wife. Therefore, headship in marriage becomes corrupted when a man fails to care for his wife the way Christ cares for the church. Besides, every husband is the ambassador for Christ in their home, just as all believers are ambassadors for Christ.

Christ's most significant responsibility to the church was to become her Saviour. So, every Christian husband has the responsibility to secure his wife and children and also prepare them against the looming judgment of the ungodly. Therefore, your family is your first mission field as a husband. You must represent Christ as a saviour.

As I understand headship more deeply, I admit that I am not the head but a representative of the Head. Even though Christ confers headship on every Christian husband, I cannot but act as the ambassador of the One who entrusted me with a home.

Describing Christ's position over creation, Apostle Paul wrote:

"He is before all things, and in him, all things hold together. And he is the head of the body, the church; he is the beginning and the firstborn from among the dead, so that in everything he might have the supremacy"- Colossians 1:17-18.

So, Christ is the Head of all things, including you- the head of your home. This means no husband is qualified to head his wife if Christ is not heading him. Every Christian husband remains relevant in their home as they submit themselves to the authority of Christ.

Creation rebelled against man after the fall because man rebelled against God first. Any man who fails to acknowledge and submit under Christ's headship will also fail to receive the honour and submission they should receive. If you lose Christ, you lose headship in marriage. Christ remains the centre focus.

Submission is a serious demand that must not be misdirected. Only a correct head can earn absolute submission. Most Christian husbands disobey God in many ways but expect their wives to submit to them in everything. They do not consider that when a man dishonours Christ, he gets shame.

Little wonder, several husbands cannot resist Satan in their homes. We receive our authority over demons from Christ. We lose our authority over evil spirits when we fail to submit to Christ.

Consider how Apostle James stated it: *"Submit yourselves, then, to God. Resist the devil, and he will flee from you."* As a Christian husband, you command both spiritual and physical submission, not by subjugation, but by submitting to Christ- the Head of all things.

Headship is Responsibility

Headship is primarily a position of responsibility and secondarily a position of authority. Conversely, several husbands want to assume the position of the commander-in-chief of their homes. Although the position of authority in every marriage belongs to the husband, I have found that you will only gain more authority as you take on more responsibility.

A man who does not provide, protect, or care for his family is on the verge of losing his headship. The reason is not far-fetched: he has failed to take responsibility. I have never found anywhere in Scripture where Jesus enforced His disciples to do anything. In fact, they retained the choice to quit following the Master. But none of the twelve disciples turned from following Christ. The reason was that Jesus took full responsibility for them.

When several people renounced Jesus, Peter confessed that they found no place to go but to stay with Jesus. The reason was that they knew that ONLY Christ has the word of life (John 6:68-69). As you take responsibility for your home, your wife and children will desire no other person or place. They will realise they won't get the love, attention, and care you offer anywhere else. Without restraint, you will win your wife's absolute submission.

While comparing the husband's role to Christ's, Paul highlighted the following:

"Husbands, love your wives, just as Christ loved the church and gave himself up for her to make her holy, cleansing her by the washing with water through the word, and to present her to himself as a radiant church, without stain or wrinkle or any other blemish, but holy and blameless. In the same way, husbands should love their wives as their own bodies. He who loves his wife loves himself"- Ephesians 5:25-28.

Christ's headship over the church is reflected in the enormous responsibility He bore. He gave up His life for the church, cleansed her impurities, and presented her to Himself as a glorious church, void of spots and wrinkles. Now, you know it is your responsibility to culture and cultivate your wife and bring out the best in her. If you find any deficiency, it is your duty to wash her, cleanse her and present her to yourself as a glorious bride. Instead of complaining about what she lacks, supply them. Build her character, nurture her body, invest in her and watch her become spotless.

One Head, One Body

Imagine a body with many heads or many bodies with just a head. That pictures a monster, right? A wife becomes monstrous when she submits to many heads, and a husband becomes monstrous when he wants to rule every woman. It is clear in Scripture that the husband is the head of his wife. While the husband acts as the head, the wife functions as the body, so one body fits perfectly into the head.

"For the husband is the head of the wife..." (Eph. 5:23).

A husband is ONLY the head of his wife and not the head of all women. In marriage, headship is confined to individual families. Never exercise headship beyond your home; otherwise, you will be trespassing. Some ministers or pastors have tried to rule over other people's wives and got their homes into a serious mess. The role of a shepherd is not the same as the role of a husband. Ministers of the gospel must be careful not to go beyond their boundaries to force women to act contrary to their husband's instructions.

No man is pleased with anyone who counsels his wife to disobey him. So, every man should understand that he is head over his home and not overall women. God does not permit headship in marriage to extend beyond individual families. If only some older men would hearken to God's word, they would cease to control their son's marriage. You are a head over your wife, not your daughter-in-law. So, every husband should maintain their God-given boundary for peace to reign.

Common Misconceptions about Headship

Headship Equals Authoritarianism

The most common misconception is that headship and control are synonymous. A few people interpret this as giving a husband the right to dismiss his wife's views and discard her opinions.

Yet the biblical ideal of headship calls husbands to a degree of mutuality and mutual submission

(Ephesians 5:21), in which both couples regard each other's input and presence.

Christ never dominated His disciples. Instead, He won their submission through His sacrificial love and mutual respect. It was not recorded that Jesus threatened His followers. He had what it takes to dominate over them: the miracles He performed were enough to bring them under subjugation, but He called them friends and brothers.

Headship is Cultural, Not Biblical

People who argue against the biblical concept of headship propose that no such headship teachings should continue because they belong to an outdated culture. The concept of headship indeed slows down change due to patriarchy's cultural mechanisms. Nevertheless, the biblical texts on headship must be considered theologically, not only historically.

Therefore, headship has no limits based on culture, and it is a call to build relationships out of love and respect rather than in line with these cultures. Marriage is God's idea, not a cultural thought. Patterning your marriage according to

God's ordinance requires biblical guidelines, not cultural assumptions or norms.

Headship Inhibits Female Empowerment

Another myth is that stressing headship automatically lessens the wife's role and contributions. The Bible includes women leaders such as Deborah and Priscilla, who served God's purpose. Though married, these women didn't lose their identity in God.

In a strong marriage, both heads, the husband and the wife, flourish by working together, and hence, headship is not confining to the woman but rather encourages her to be an active participant in the marriage.

Headship Means a Lack of Responsibility

Some see headship as an opportunity to release oneself from obligations toward the relationship. Yet, according to Scripture, headship carries a call to accountability in all types of relationships and to spiritual leadership. He is responsible for the spiritual health of his family, including creating conditions under which faith is cultivated and preserved.

Adam, the first man and husband, was dutiful before God found him qualified for marriage. Failing to take responsibility is the earliest symptom of a man losing his headship position.

CHAPTER 3

THE SIGNIFICANCE

Every part of the body is important, each with its unique identity and role. Different cells unite to form a tissue, several tissues combine to produce an organ, and the collaboration of unique organs makes up our body system. This means that a cell has a significant role in the body. By this, we understand that every part of the body is unique. However, some parts of the body play more roles than others.

For instance, the head consists of the brain, which controls every cerebral function, such as thoughts and emotions. The head governs the movement of the entire body and connects the body to the senses of sight, hearing, taste, and smell. Moreover, the head represents an individual's identity.

During vital registrations or applications, you are often required to submit or upload a passport photograph, which only shows the head region. This is because a human head accurately represents the entire body. Now you understand why most criminals wear masks to hide their true identity from being captured by CCTV or their victims.

The head of any organisation is sufficient to represent the entire organisation in any meeting or conference. Sometimes, only the head of a company is sent for training. He or she is believed to pass the knowledge to every organisation member in the long run. All these illustrations substantiate headship's significance in any institution- including marriage.

All-encompassing

The more we examine Christ's responsibility to the church, the clearer we see who an ideal husband is. Scripturally, we learn that Christ is the Head of all things and that all things fit into Him (Col. 1:17).

He was in heaven, came down to earth, was buried beneath, went down into hell, and ascended into the heavens, where He sits at the Father's right hand. He fills all things- He is all-inclusive (Eph. 1:23).

In 2020, the Lord opened my understanding of a husband's all-encompassing role. Since then, I admit that every husband's responsibility is all-encompassing.

Right within my heart, the Lord said: "How many sense organs do you have?" Quickly and without mincing words, I responded, "Five." He asked again: "How many sense organs consist in the head?"

Immediately, I understood what the Lord was calling my attention to. I was only a student fellowship pastor at that time. We were preparing for a brothers and sisters' weekend—a relationship-centered meeting that held every session. However, the Lord was preparing me for my marriage. Now, I understand better. Thanks to God, I treasured His word.

Only the head contains all five sense organs in the whole body. Minus the head, every other body part only feels and reacts. But the head contains the eyes, which connect the body to the organ of sight.

The nose enables the sense of smell; the ears activate our ability to hear and observe sounds, and the tongue actuates our ability to taste and differentiate sweet, sour, and bitter substances.

Plus, the head is covered with skin, which also feels like every other part of the body.

Apart from hosting all the sense organs, the head houses the brain, which coordinates all cognitive actions. A man can survive if he loses a leg or hand. One of the most delicate parts of the body is the spinal cord. However, people have survived without their spinal cords in place. But no one survives if his head is cut off.

As a husband, you are an indispensable entity in your home. You need to let this truth settle deep into you. When a man divorces his wife and leaves her to cater for the children alone, he causes untold damage to those children. It's disheartening to x-ray the effects of a broken home or a home where the man of the house fails to take responsibility.

Imagine what pain your body would go through if your eyes ceased to function for three days. You will subject your family to greater torture if you fail to see their spiritual, physical, and emotional needs. They would stagger through life because of your spiritual and emotional insensitivity.

Unfortunately, the blindness of a man will greatly affect his wife and children. Achan's blindness prevented him from seeing the danger of disobeying God's order. Consequently, he perished with his wife and children (Jos. 7:24-26).

Nabal's inability to see ahead would have destroyed his entire home but for the wisdom of his wife, Abigail (1 Sam. 25:2-38). He couldn't smell the looming danger over his life and family. Nabal was an apology of a head- a callous and insensitive husband.

You are the head of your home. You are responsible for seeing, hearing, tasting, tasting, and feeling. Just as the head cannot shift the sense of sight to the hand, there are responsibilities you shouldn't shift to your wife.

If the eyes go blind, the hands can grope in darkness to guide the body, just like a blind man would use a walking stick to aid movement. Unfortunately, this is what some women are experiencing in their marriages. They have taken the responsibility of their husbands.

Patience is Key

Besides the head, every other body part only feels and reacts to stimuli. This is one of the reasons women are more emotional and reactive than men. Sometimes, you could see farther than your wife. You could picture what tomorrow may bring, but your wife is mostly concerned about today's needs.

For an analogy, you might be trying to cut down expenses to save for eventualities. Your wife could develop a negative interpretation of your actions because she has an immediate desire. It takes patience for you to handle such a situation.

Sometimes, you can face a challenge that your wife might need help understanding. When finances are down, and you have several needs to meet, she might become resentful. Don't take things too personally; she is only skin and has to react to stimuli. No healthy individual will not respond when pinched with a needle.

Sarah suggested her maid to Abraham when she considered that she was barren and aged. But when Hagar became pregnant, Sarah dragged Abraham for her predicament. Such could be the situation sometimes, especially when the man of the house fails to see ahead. I wonder what would be running through Father Abraham's mind then.

I am more surprised that Abraham didn't accuse his wife of luring him into adultery. He took responsibility for his actions. Plus, he knew that Sarah had just the sense of feeling and had to react to her pains. She didn't admit she was the chief cause of her husband's action.

It requires patience and divine wisdom to navigate through knotty situations. This is why every Christian husband must activate all their spiritual senses to ensure they do not act under undue influence, come what may. With wisdom, we can communicate God's plan to our wives in difficult times and comfort them to be patient until God comes to our rescue.

Do not give up or act in resentment when your best is not appreciated. The Lord sees your heart and will reward you. He will also bind your family together with the cord of love.

You see, Jesus didn't give up because He was ridiculed by the people He came to save. He died with the hope that they would repent. Today, we are partakers of eternal salvation because Christ endured suffering. With time, your spouse and children will realise how much you love and sacrifice for them.

Take full responsibility

Since all the sense organs consist of the head, every husband must take full responsibility for their home without grumbling. This can be a very bitter pill, but admitting it is better. I do not imply that husbands should bear burdens alone while their wives sit idle at home. All husbands should be responsible for their homes because they are accountable to God.

Headship means you must gain the total capacity to manage your home without defaulting in any area (1 Tim. 3:4-5). Let it be that your wife's role is supportive or complementary. Remember that God gave Eve as a helper to Adam (Gen. 2:18), so Adam was the main worker while Eve played a supportive role. The day Eve attempted headship, the entire human race started suffering for it. She engaged in a dialogue with the Serpent, which was disastrous.

When God came into the garden and found that Adam and Eve had disobeyed His instructions, He called Adam to account. God wasn't oblivious that the whole calamity began with Eve. He questioned Adam because he positioned him as the head of the family. I wish Adam had taken responsibility for the rebellion.

Maybe God's judgment would have changed if Adam had crumbled on his knees and cried for mercy. Instead, he played the blame game. God questioned Adam first in His infinite wisdom but judged him last (Gen. 3:9-24).

Adam's punishment was more severe than Eve's because he failed to take responsibility. Eli had a taste of the consequence of failing to take responsibility, too. He wasn't corrupt, but his children were. When God called his attention to his failure, he asked God to do as He pleased (1 Samuel 3:18). God did as he said.

We must work and take charge of our homes as men who must give account. You will not just answer for yourself; you will also give an account of your stewardship over your household. This is why God made you the head and gave you all the senses necessary to perform your duties effectively.

You may need to ask God to activate your spiritual, physical, financial, and emotional senses so you won't perform below His expectations.

CHAPTER 4
LOVE: THE HALLMARK OF HEADSHIP

Since the task of headship is enormous, it is impossible to perform it outside the boundary of love. Little wonder God commands every husband to love their wives (Eph. 5:25). Love is the greatest commandment for all.

However, within the confines of marriage, God specifically mandates husbands to love their wives exceptionally and unconditionally. This is because love will grease off every friction associated with your headship function. So, instead of grumbling, you will derive joy in performing your duties.

God didn't command wives to love their husbands. He instructed them to submit to their husbands as to the Lord. Well, I hope you understand that God didn't license wives to hate their husbands. Naturally, it is easier for a woman to love her husband than to submit to him. But a man finds it difficult to love because it is an enormous task trying to understand a woman.

A gospel minister once counselled men not to try to understand their wives. He said they should love her whether they understood her or not. Humorously, he added that a man can never understand his wife because he was asleep when God formed her. That's funny, but you see, women are unique. They think, act, and react differently from men. But we can always win them over with love.

Christ-like Love

"Husbands, love your wives, just as Christ loved the church and gave himself up for her"

- Ephesians 5:25

Everyone has a value system. We choose what we want and decide what we love. Some habits and characters attract us to people, while others we have developed zero tolerance for. Most of us love people based on certain conditions. When those conditions are not met, we overswitch to dislike them.

Each time I study how God wants me to love my wife, I consider that I do not have a choice of how to love her other than how the word of God prescribes it. It would still be a complete thought if the Bible passage ended with, *"Husbands, love your wives."* But God knows that some of our value systems are not in tandem with His holy word.

Any husband that God will approve must not only love his wife. He must do so, *"just as Christ loved the church and gave himself up for her."* As we deeply study how much Christ bestows love on His church, we will understand what it truly means for husbands to love their wives. Simply put, you can't love your wife however you want and win God's approval. You have to love her the way Christ loves the church.

To what extent is the love of Christ for the church?

"But God demonstrates his own love for us in this: While we were still sinners, Christ died for us"- Romans 5:8.

Christ's love outweighs our sins. He didn't see the weight of our transgression as enough reason to abandon us in our depravity. He died for our sins when we were most unworthy of divine pardon. Who would die for a worthless, unrepentant criminal but Christ? O God!

Christ didn't love us because we repented. He didn't die for our sins because we showed interest in Him. He laid down His life as a sacrifice for our iniquities because He loves us unconditionally. So, I have learned to hate sin and love sinners because Christ died for me while I was still in my sins.

Now that God commands us to love our wives the same way Christ loves His church, it means that no condition or boundary should be attached to our love for our spouses. If indeed we live in obedience to the word of God, then we will find no offence too enormous to forgive. If Christ died for you when you were most unworthy, then you should love your wife when she seems most underserving.

Love and Submission

I once heard a man say to his wife, "You can't have my love if I can't have your submission." I knew the gentleman was trying to play smart. He remained disobedient to God's command. You see, God never said that husbands should love their wives if they submit. Neither did the Bible say that wives should submit to their husbands only when they are most loving.

In marriage, love and submission are unconditional. We get into a mess when we manoeuvre God's word to suit our selfish desires. If only men love their wives unconditionally, and every woman submits to their husbands as to the Lord, most marriage problems will efface.

Here is the balance: although love and submission are unconditional in marriage, joy, intimacy, and fulfilment are highly conditional. If your wife submits to you but you fail to love her as God commands, you are ripping off her joy and the sense of fulfilment she deserves. The same thing happens when a man loves his wife, but she fails to submit to him.

However, if you desire a positive change in your home, it is better that the change begins with you. Instead of accusing your wife of not submitting to you, scale up your love for her. Loving your wife is the best way to win her submission. Usually, women submit to their husbands when their love tank is full.

We are to love our wives, not as we would want to, but as Christ loves the church. With this divine instruction, we can truly admit that love is a debt we can never exhaust paying. You cannot love your wife too much; this is true because the greatest proof of love is sacrifice (John 15:13).

CHAPTER 5

HEADING WITH KNOWLEDGE

"In the same way you married men should live considerately with [your wives], with an intelligent recognition [of the marriage relation], honouring the woman as [physically] the weaker, but [realising that you] are joint heirs of the grace (God's unmerited favour) of life, in order that your prayers may not be hindered and cut off. [Otherwise you cannot pray effectively.]

- 1 Peter 3:7 (AMP).

In most industries and establishments, new workers are usually trained and allowed to familiarise themselves with the ethics of their workplace. The onboarding ensures that individual workers possess the requisite knowledge of the company and their roles. Additionally, most organisations conduct regular workshops and development programmes to enhance their workers' understanding. These regular training sessions keep the workers fit and productive to meet their company's expectations.

Similarly, every Christian husband should learn their wives in order to relate with them accordingly. When knowledge is lacking, misunderstanding and meaningless arguments are inevitable. But where abundant knowledge is in place, peace and joy abound.

Oneness and sameness are two distinct realities in marriage. Until death, a man and his wife will always think and act differently; sometimes, their opinions are convergent and sometimes divergent. This understanding allows you to maximise your diversity while living with your wife. Unity in diversity is one of the greatest mysteries of marriage.

Your physical and emotional needs are different from your wife's. Moreover, you may not possess the same temperaments. Borrowing from Gary Chapman, your love languages may be different. The differences in age, beliefs, experiences, perceptions, and upbringing can create some mental gaps. However, knowledge can help bridge the gap.

Honouring Your Spouse

It is not only wives that should honour their husbands. Both husbands and wives should honour themselves. Honour flows naturally when a man loves his wife and when a wife submits to her husband. God's word commands every man to live considerately with his wife. Honouring her should stem from an intelligent recognition of the marriage union and the awareness of her physical weakness.

No man should take advantage of his wife's physical weakness to assault her. Instead, your physical strength should be to protect her. Marriage brings you and your wife into oneness regardless of your political, academic, social, or financial status. Honour her with your body and possessions with the knowledge that anyone who loves his wife loves himself (Eph. 5:28).

Maybe you think your wife should know more than she does. But remember that she is a weaker vessel which must be accorded honour. If you accept her weakness, you will find her strength. Besides, if you fail to dwell with her according to knowledge, there will be a crisis in your home.

Formidable Synergy

"Two are better than one, because they have a good return for their labor: If either of them falls down, one can help the other up. But pity anyone who falls down, and no one has to help them up. Also, if two lie down together, they will keep warm. But how can one keep warm alone? Though one may be overpowered, two can defend themselves. A cord of three strands is not quickly broken."

- Ecclesiastes 4:9-12

Over and again, I have found this passage to be true in my marriage. Debby will encourage me when I tend to be weak spiritually. There is hardly any night she doesn't intercede for me. Sometimes, as we lie in bed, she places her hand gently on me and speaks quietly in tongues. I have found strength because I am not alone.

There were times when my wife cautioned me not to make certain decisions. I have been grateful for considering her counsel. When the going gets tough, I find strength in her. God made it so because He loves intimacy. He doesn't only want us to relate with Him as a spiritual

Being; He also provides an ambience of physical and emotional intimacy through marriage.

The synergy of a husband and wife whose faith rests absolutely in Christ produced effectual results. If every husband and wife can live in the unity of faith, they will move mountains and achieve the seemingly unachievable. It is confirmed in God's word that one will chase a thousand, but the synergy of two will put ten thousand enemies to flight (Deut. 32:30). That is the force and fire God intends marriage to generate.

However, Satan, the accuser of brethren- hates godly relationships. He does all within his capacity to break any union that hosts God's presence. That Old Serpent was the first to break spirit-spirit, spirit-human, and human-human relationship. He destroyed the relationship between God and one-third of the heavenly angels (Rev. 12:9).

After he was cast out of heaven, he corrupted the relationship between God, Adam and Eve. Thereafter, he stirred Cain against his brother Abel, and he murdered him. Satan achieved these in succession. Up till now, he is still destroying good relationships- spiritual and physical.

The increasing rate of divorce in our day tells how tirelessly Satan is still in the business of scattering relationships. Unfortunately, some Christians have allowed the devil into their homes. Several homes have been scattered while many other couples are only cohabiting; the joy of intimacy has long departed from them.

Take a Stand against Satan

The Scripture equips us with so much knowledge of God to discern Satan's devices. As you live with your spouse, you need to take a stand against Satan. One of the things you must know is that the devil wishes to destroy your home. That is why we are enjoined to be watchful and vigilant, because Satan- our adversary, is like a roaring lion seeking whom to devour (1Pet. 5:8).

Satan is always seeking opportunities to cause division between you and your spouse. Sometimes, he wants to take advantage of your differences. He amplifies your wife's shortcomings to make you detest everything about her. It is you that must be watchful not to allow Satan into your home.

Meditate on 1Peter 3:7 again:

*"Husbands, in the same way, be considerate as you live with your wives, and treat them with respect as the weaker partner and as heirs with you of the precious gift of life, **so that nothing will hinder your prayers.**"*

If you fail to dwell with your wife according to knowledge, you may risk your prayers being unanswered. God does not dwell where disunity exists. So, you must consciously and deliberately avoid everything and anything that can cause division between you and your spouse.

To pray effectively, you must learn to forgive your spouse. Jesus told us that God will not forgive us or answer our prayers until we have forgiven our offenders- including our spouses (Mark 11:25-26). Offences are inevitable, so you must prepare against them. If your spouse offends you, harmlessly communicate your pain and forgive her. This way, you are keeping the devil away from your home.

Are you tired of your marriage? Do you feel like calling it quits? God can spark the fire of love in your home again. He will give you the wisdom you need to address every situation. Your prayers can keep the devil away and genuinely reunite you with your wife.

CHAPTER 6

SPIRITUAL LEADERSHIP IN THE HOME

"Start children off on the way they should go, and even when they are old they will not turn from it"

-Proverbs 22:6

On a particular day, while working with my dad in a cornfield, I said, "Thank you, Dad, for training us in the way of the Lord." I was so sure of my conviction to follow Christ. If my dad had led us down the wrong path, it might have been tough for me to accept Jesus as my Saviour.

My zeal for the Lord might have been diverted to the pursuit of worldly passions and temporary things. However, I am exposed to the love of Christ through daily family devotions, children's Sunday school classes in our local church, and several other Christian camp meetings.

Although my New Birth experience began at age 14, I have always been conscious of Bible teachings and parental instructions. These were courtesy of my dad's spiritual leadership in our home. He ensured we prayed daily and observed special Christian holidays, apart from our consistent engagement with the local church we attended.

In Christianity, domestic spiritual leadership is the ability to lead family members toward God. A husband needs to be a priest of his own home, and that means he is constantly active in nurturing a healthy relationship with God through prayer, reading Scripture, and engaging in ministries. Such fundamental spiritual concepts in a husband's life serve as a motivating example for the whole family.

Faith Modelling

The primary responsibility of a husband in the context of spiritual leadership is to model the faith. This means being a doer of the word and not just a hearer and living the tenets one wants to teach the family. For instance, the husband may not only go to church services every Sunday or lead religious activities but also display such values as kindness and compassion to others. This particularly concerns the husband's behaviour as it illustrates the belief.

Family members, most especially children, tend to be keen spectators of some of the parents' activities. Children can also take cues from a man who is always on the floor praying or reading the Bible, and this quite often motivates them. So, the husband's zeal for faith is a major factor in shaping the spiritual atmosphere within the household.

As a husband, be the first to model the life you want your wife and children to live. Children tend to emulate their parents' actions rather than obey their words. So, what you do will affect you and your children.

In the end, leading in a spiritual way has little to do with teaching someone to do something. A husband serves as an example to the family when he does his best to practice what is consistent with spirituality. If a husband practices virtues such as patience, kindness, integrity, faithfulness, and many others, he stands as an example of those virtues in action, and such a man can motivate and empower his family members.

Building a Faith-Based Environment in the Home

Another role of a husband is creating an ambience that allows spirituality to be practiced beyond mere activity. This entails integrating spiritual practices into the family's operational activities, such as praying before meals, sharing Bible verses, and engaging in moral entertainment. In this way, devotee fathers ensure that the practice of religion remains active and natural to all family members.

Furthermore, to help reinforce certain spiritual principles in the home, creating family traditions based on spirituality, where certain holidays are celebrated in a significant way, or doing certain activities that help the community during that period can be helpful as well.

Encouraging Personal Growth

In spiritual leadership, a husband plays an important part in cultivating every family member's personal spiritual growth. This means he must also encourage his wife on her spiritual path and educate his children in matters of faith.

Such encouragement can be geared in different ways, including discussing the Scripture, suggesting some growth-enhancing literature, or just being there to listen and address one's concerns.

My dad is a dedicated reader of Christian literature. I learned that from him. Now, in his late seventies, he still studies the Bible and reads Christian novels. He was bold enough to encourage us to study our Bibles and pray because he was doing the same.

In addition to leading in spiritual matters, effective spiritual leadership also calls for a husband to promote the spirit of togetherness and communication within the family. This includes leading in prayer and engaging families in expressing their views and feelings regarding faith. In this way, the husband plays the role of ensuring that everyone present speaks and that such discussions do not become one directive instruction but are participative in nature.

Disputes will cling to every relationship, and it is in these circumstances that the contribution of spiritual leadership is paramount. A husband should attempt to resolve conflicts, whenever possible, in a softer and considerate tone, and whenever conflict is escalated, to find a solution that teaches Christian values of forgiveness, love and patience. All of this reinforces the family's spirit and is an active example of dealing with problems that arise in faith.

Belonging to a Local Church/Community Support

Taking on a spiritual leadership role as a husband applies not only to the family but also to other communities of believers. Participating in church functions, volunteering, and community projects can help enhance the family's spiritual environment and stress the need to serve and help others.

This involvement impacts the family because they learn what constitutes a community and how to rely on each other, fulfilling the biblical command to love your neighbour.

In addition, husbands' devotion to the community serves as a catalyst for the family to take action. They can participate in missions, charitable activities, and other families' fellowships, and thus, they are able to grow in faith as a unit.

Establishing an Everyday Spiritual Routine

Establishing a spiritual calendar and practices in one's home does not require complex systems or elaborate practices. On the contrary, it can be a part of everyday life that creates memorable and remarkable spiritual moments.

You can consider some of the following schedules in your daily routine to assist the family in growing spiritually.

Morning Commitments: Beginning the Day with Intent

Mornings can positively influence the rest of the day. A brief family devotion, prayer, or meditation session helps draw attention to spirituality. Such may include reading a scripture that commends a verse, sharing an insight or two on the verse, and outlining an agenda for the day.

By engaging God in the early hours of each day, you are teaching your family the need to prioritise God. Instilling such spiritual values also allows your family to appreciate the essence of the day ahead and be purposely geared towards it.

Mealtime Blessings: A Moment for Reflection

Meal time offers an opportunity for all those present to appreciate spiritual and family togetherness. You can offer a gentle request encouraging everyone to pray before eating. This practice addresses the need for bonding and allows for discussing appreciation, challenges, and faith within the everyday bustle.

Appreciating God before the meal is a good way to follow the practice of Christ, who always gives thanks to the Father at the table. On one or two occasions, Jesus gave thanks to God, and the little supply available miraculously multiplied to feed five thousand men, women, and children. This shows that mealtime blessings are a scriptural practice that should be encouraged in our homes.

Open Discussions: Creating Opportunity for Conversations

Having open and honest discussions about spirituality is crucial. In so doing, husbands can encourage family members to share their life experiences and even the challenges faced in relation to faith and share the scriptures. Help them to ask questions, which will be the starting point of their spiritual growth.

When you create a safe environment for family members to share their faith and ask questions, you will record exponential spiritual growth. This is because everyone feels safe to share their beliefs without fear of attack.

Moreover, open discussions help you discover areas where you need to be more supportive of your family members. As you discover areas where their beliefs do not align with Scripture, it is easier to correct them in love.

Evening Reflection: Time to Relax and Bond with the Family

Recall the day by spending time with the family at the end of the day. This may comprise narrating the day's experiences, highlighting certain events, or sharing spiritual stories.

A husband may lead this time by sharing thoughts from the heart concerning matters of faith and urging other family members to do the same. This practice will enhance spiritual bonds and help cope with life's highs and lows with hope and faith.

By leading your family to God at the beginning and end of each day, they will learn to make God the Alpha and Omega and the Author and Finisher of their faith.

The Strains of Leadership

The responsibilities of a wholesome husband are heavy and hard to bear. Work, family, and social duties leave little, if any, room for reflection. Consequently, it may be impossible for many husbands to play their role of spiritual leader, creating an imbalance in 'what is needed' and 'what is able' regarding leadership.

Time Constraints

The pull and push of everyday existence are conducive to the adverse scheduling of spiritual practices. At stages of life when workload and caregiving responsibilities increase multitasking, the opportunity to pray, read scriptures or even talk about spirituality is non-existent, leaving husbands ready to lead their families spiritually but completely unarmed.

Relational Dynamics

Spiritual leadership is not only personal but requires the collaboration and participation of all family members. A husband may face opposition, dissent, and indifference from the family members, disrupting his ability to practice certain spiritual activities. This can be disheartening, especially if he feels that he has no one to turn to for support.

Self-Confidence Issues

Most husbands have to cope with unrealistic expectations concerning how much spirituality they should practice and their capacity to lead. They fear failing either to themselves or to what society expects, which makes them avoid being in the forefront. Because of this lack of confidence, these men are usually hesitant about leading any spiritual program or even starting spiritual conversations, which leads to no spiritual life within the family.

These days, when spirituality is most often pushed out of the limelight, husbands are found to have the duty of internalising their religion. They may also wonder how they can share their true religious feelings without being considered impostors or one-sided in beliefs.

Practical Approaches to Spiritual Leadership

Despite these challenges, there are practical strategies husbands can embrace to become more effective spiritual leaders in their homes:

Live by Example

The most advantageous way a husband can exert his leadership in the spiritual aspect is through devoted practice on a personal level. This does not mean one has to be perfect; instead, it stresses the need to be honest, sincerely present, and willing to change.

When you pray, read the Bible, and talk about faith regularly, you set a good example for the whole family. By walking the talk, your life becomes worthy of emulation.

Making a Spiritual Schedule for the Family

Some aspects of spirituality can be incorporated into one's daily life to some degree by embracing practices such as family prayers, reading the Bible, or going to church as a family. These activities help create a bond and enable family members to express and share their feelings regarding spirituality.

If your local church is spiritually healthy, your family will learn more from the church leaders about the areas where their beliefs conflict with the Scripture.

Filling the Self's Internal Reservoir

It is crucial for husbands to take their spiritual growth seriously. This may involve attending meetings, being part of a book club, reading religious texts, or even getting a spiritual mentor/disciple. Knowledge of their beliefs reinforces their faith and prepares them for effective leadership.

If you fail to develop yourself, your family will lose trust in your leadership ability. But by filling your internal reservoir, you will have more to dispense daily for the growth of your home.

Join a Community of Believers

Everybody can benefit from being part of a church or a group of couples with similar interests. These communities provide support, motivation, and control. It is easier to face challenges knowing that others have gone through similar experiences.

You will find strength and support in your local church or other committed group of believers. The testimony of other successful men in marriage will help you stay focused and hopeful.

It is indisputable that a husband's role as a spiritual leader within the family is not a walk in the park. However, the leadership position offers an opportunity that can positively influence the spiritual well-being of the family and their togetherness.

Always draw strength from the word of God as you take responsibility for your home. Know that God is the Supplier of every resource marriage requires to thrive. So, do not lean on your understanding. Instead, ask the Holy Spirit to help you raise godly seeds and nurture a home where Christ is reverenced and served.

FINAL THOUGHTS

Every Christian husband occupies a noble office that comes with an enormous responsibility. However, ruling our homes becomes easier when the word of God guides us. As we reach the final pages of this book, I encourage you to reflect on the following questions: Have you submitted yourself under God's headship? How can you rate your success in performing your headship role in your home? Have you lost your value as the head of your family, or are you struggling to retain it?

If your answer to any of the questions suggests that you must make amends, God will restore and help you build the home he has assigned you. However, you must repent and invite God into your home. Let the word of God be your guide. Do not place societal values above the Scripture. You will find help as you submit yourself under God's authority.

Importantly, every husband needs to develop themselves in many areas to fit into their headship office. You might need to establish yourself financially, spiritually, or emotionally to retain your value in your home. Besides, you should unlearn some values that have negatively impacted your marriage and learn values that promote love and intimacy.

If you follow God's standard for a Christian marriage, ensure it does not derail from scriptural paths. Do not allow undue influences to erode the word of God from your heart. A marriage that will stand the test of time requires commitment. Be prayerful to discern the tactics of Satan when he comes around your marriage.

As the head of your family, the best legacy you can leave is to lead your family to Christ and train your children in the way of the Lord. Engage your family in spiritual things. Pray together. Study God's word together. Attend a local church together and give your best to God's service. Your children will learn and take after you. God will also be proud to have entrusted lives into your care.

Remember that headship in marriage is not about dominance but mutual submission to God's will. When husbands and wives grasp this truth, their relationships transform. You and your spouse can become unstoppable, reflecting God's love and redeeming the world.